BLUEPRINTING

for Successful Self-Publishing

by

SHARON D. ANDERSON, Ph.D.

Angelic Communications

Cape Cod, MA 02632

Digital Rights Reserved

ISBN – 13: 978-1717233981

ISBN – 10: 1717233988

"Nothing is impossible. The word itself says,
'I'm possible'."

~~ Audrey Hepburn

ACKNOWLEDGMENTS

A special thank you to the members of the Cape Cod Writers Studio.

I wrote it for them

Also

Thank you to my Angels and Guides who insisted that I write it and "book" it.

They kept me up nights working on it by the light of the silvery moon. (no pun intended)

Don't you just love 'em?

Contents

Welcome to Blueprinting for Successful Self-Publishing

Two questions writers ask about their manuscript are:

1. How do I publish it?

2. How do I market it (sell it)?

To answer your first question, you have two options: You can try to have it published by the traditional route – which means writing query letters and sending them out to a lot of publishing houses and/or agents, OR you can self-publish your manuscript. That is what this Blueprinting is all about.

The answer to the second question is: there are many, many ways to sell your book (marketing) and we will touch on a few that might work for you. They are not blatant "sell a million books and get rich quick" but have a long-term approach.

A good definition for self-publishing is:

***"Self-publishing** is the publication of any book, album or other media by its author without the involvement of an established publisher. Unlike the traditional publishing model in which control of the publication is shared with a publisher, the author controls the entire process in a self-publishing effort including the design of the cover and the interior, price, distribution, marketing, and public relations. The authors can do all of these activities by themselves or they may outsource these tasks."*

Source – Wikipedia

Also, from Wikipedia, came this side bar of interesting predictions from a website new to me but a nice resource:

www.writtenwordmedia.com

Predictions

Most fiction sales will come from e-books

Indie authors and smaller presses will be dominant

Amazon titles will be the bestsellers

Kindle Unlimited readership will keep growing

Increased competition as market is flooded

Audiobooks will become more popular

Facebook ads will be less persuasive

International sales will spur profits

Increasingly authors will work together

Source: Chloe Smith 2017

https://www.writtenwordmedia.com/2017/01/04/top-ten-trends-in-publishing-every-author-needs-to-know-in-2017/

And this quote:

"For decades, the literary world dismissed self-published authors as amateurs and hacks who lacked the talent to land a book deal. But that attitude gradually began to change with the rise of e-books and the arrival of Kindle from Amazon, which gave authors direct access to millions of readers."

— Alexandra Alter in the New York Times, 2016

An excellent summary of the self-publishing world over the last 20 years…

Self-Publishing isn't easy, it takes demanding work and dedication, as my students will tell you now that they are well into the task.

Your thoughts

One of the questions you should ask yourself is:

What are my expectations after I publish my book?

Self-Publishing is not a "get rich quick scheme", although there are many authors who will sell you their book proclaiming that if you follow what they tell you, you will.

Yes, you'll sell copies of your book to friends and relations, and a few at the local bookstore. If you do a book signing, you will sell some there. Then what?

Is your focus just on the writing and becoming a famous author? Or do you want a career in writing and publishing?

My personal focus is to use my writing and publishing skills to help other authors and writers achieve their career potential, by offering them professional self-publishing tools to create their own books, (e-book and paperback), podcasts, audio books, and have my own career as an author.

Think about what YOU really want to create as a self-publisher. The possibilities are endless.

A Paperback Process

Here is a summary of the Self-Publishing Process for a <u>paperback book</u>:

1. Idea and concept

2. Writing the story outline

3. Rewriting

.4. Story editing for plot, etc.

5. More rewriting to polish the manuscript

6. Copy editing for semi-final copy

7. Copy out to Beta Readers

8. Make any changes for final copy

9. Layout and formatting

10. Cover design

11. ISBN purchase (optional)

12. Select categories and keywords

13. Pricing

14. Distribution channels

15. Upload documents

16. Preview

17. Make changes (if any)

18. Resubmit edited copy and/or cover

19. Order proofs

20. Receive proofs and accept or make further changes

21. Order Author copies

22. Marketing and promotion

An E-Book Process

Here is the process for an <u>e-book</u>, not as involved, but still necessary.

1. Idea and concept

2. Writing the story outline

3. Rewriting

.4. Story editing for plot, etc.

5. More rewriting to polish the manuscript

6. Copy editing for semi-final copy

7. Copy out to Beta Readers (4 or 5)

8. Make any changes for final copy

9. Cover design

10. Select categories and keywords

11. Pricing

12. Distribution channels

13. Upload documents (cover and text)

14. Preview

15. Make changes (if any)

16. Resubmit edited copy and/or cover

17. Preview final copy

18. Marketing and promotion

Are you discouraged? Don't be. If you work through the process step-by-step you will end up with a terrific book. Who knows, it may be a best seller.

Back to Blueprinting

What you are reading is the most up-to-date information on successful self-publishing. The first edition of the Blueprinting was published in 2015 and 2016 in my book *Writing as a Retail Business*.

The actual art of self-publishing has not changed, the basic concepts still are the same, what has changed is the attitude towards self-publishers and the tools available to carry out those goals.

Back in 'them-thar-days', self-publishers were considered self-absorbed, egotistical vanity authors who were not worthy to be considered by a traditional publishing house. Their only choice was to pay thousands of dollars to have their well written and worthy manuscript in print.

Then, along came Amazon in 2008 and changed everything. They introduced a new way to read books. They introduced Kindle and the e-book.

Times have changed drastically since I began self-publishing in 1998. At that time, I published the church bulletin and a directory of restaurants.

Now, with Amazon and the global connection through the world wide web, anything is possible.

Amazing there are still some who feel that to self-publish is not proper, or worse, not worthy. (did you get that Bostonian accent in there?)

Where I live, we still have a few local libraries and traditional book stores that WILL NOT ACCEPT a self-published book, even though it took years to write, edit, edit again, re-write, and edit one more time so that it would be fit for human consumption.

(Warning! This is my soap-box, FYI.)

We are in the digital age, are we not? And every cell phone, iPhone, Android, Kindle, Nook, tablet, laptop, and computer have a reader attached, sometimes more than one.

Allow me to repeat this:

We are in the digital age, are we not? And every cell phone, iPhone, Android, Kindle, Nook, Tablet, Laptop, and Desk Top Computer have a reader attached, sometimes more than one.

Sorry, it just came out!

How many of you have a stack of rejection letters from traditional publishers somewhere in your closet? I always tell people I used mine to wallpaper the bathroom as a reminder to never think along traditional publishing lines again.

Self-publishing does not carry the stigma it used to. Especially now that some self-published authors are making a six-figure income from their self-publishing sites, and many have given up their day job to become full-time writers/authors.

I won't bore you anymore with the TRADITIONAL vs SELF-PUBLISHING lore, I am certain you have heard it all, but if you haven't already thought about becoming a self-published author, please consider the idea as you go along in this book. I will devote a whole section to all the benefits of self-publishing.

You must be interested in self-publishing, otherwise you wouldn't be reading or listening to this book. It will be offered in both formats. (yes, another benefit of self-publishing.)

BLUEPRINTING is exactly that, a blueprint or guide to help you create your own self-publishing business. Or simply self-publish a single manuscript if you are not quite ready to go the complete Entrepreneur route.

What you have on your device is a comprehensive Blueprint for Self-Publishing. I encourage you to read it carefully, page-by-page, section-by-section, and re-read it and listen to the audio version too.

I've covered most of what I know to date. This is a complete overview of the system I used to self-publish twenty-five books on Amazon, coach other writers to publish their work, and teach classes in self-publishing.

I truly believe if you follow this Blueprint, you can easily create an e-book and a paperback book, (even an audio book) and publish it on Amazon. This could be the beginning of your own self-publishing career, and a six-figure income.

In the very near future, I expect to receive an email from you telling me how this book on Blueprinting has changed your life, and you are now a successful self-publisher. Here's the address:

Audacious-publisher@gmail.com

<u>Authors Note:</u>

Although this book can be read as pure text, it is best to read it on a tablet or computer to click through the links for extra material

This document is Copyright by the Audacious-Publisher.com

If you find it useful, please share it with anyone else who might be interested in this information.

You have my permission to embed it on your blog, share it with your writers group, or on a forum or anywhere you like, email it to a friend or use excerpts on your site, providing you cite the source and don't sell the content.

Thank you,

The Audacious Publisher

How I became a self-published author.

Not unlike your own story, I had been publishing church bulletins, then a dining directory (because I was new to the area and had no clue where the delicious food was). In this process, I learned to use several self-publishing programs. I also did a lot of other ventures, too. I won't bore you with those details. After wading through a pile of unsuccessful attempts in other ventures, I decided to write my own book. I had my doctorate in the field of metaphysics, which was my then current field of expertise, but was still fascinated with the writing and publishing aspects of the computer age. I was hooked.

I had been doing a lot of research on writing and read somewhere in a book this tiny bit of advice: *'write about what you know.'*

Well, that was easy. I knew all about Angels and the Angelic Realm, so that is what I wrote about. At that time, no publishing house was interested in books about angels. The rejection slips were piling up and I was getting frustrated. (I still write about them, my Something Series; *Something Sinister, Something Bloody and Something Lov-er-ly)*

I was finally directed to BookLocker.com, who accepted my manuscript and I had my first book. *Angels in Action.*

I published four more books with them. This process was considered 'self-publishing', and although inexpensive as far as the industry of publishing houses, it was still costly.

My lifestyle changed, (I retired at that age of 65 and so did my income.) In 2009, I discovered KDP, a new subsidiary of Amazon who was making great strides in digital publishing, introducing the Kindle Reader,

(Kindle Direct Publishing) and I have been with them ever since.

I recommend Amazon and work with them exclusively.

Amazon is the perfect venue for a newbie to begin their career in self-publishing, especially when you are just starting out and have limited income to invest.

In 2016, I founded the Cape Cod Writers Studio to help other writers learn how to publish their books on Amazon. We meet weekly at a local library to polish our manuscripts and eventually publish them. The Studio has been open for almost two years and four students have self-published, with two more in process. See my website for their success stories:

www.audacious-publisher.com

Self-Publishing as a business, not a hobby.

When you publish your first book, either e-book or print, you have created INVENTORY. Yup, you now have a product to sell. You are 'in business' as my parents used to say.

To be 'in business', you need a market place, somewhere to sell your inventory. You already have one and are using it now. Yes, the WWW or world wide web. This is your market place. Eventually, you will need to set up a 'storefront' in which to sell your books (Your website).

If you are familiar with social media and Facebook, you can create a Facebook business page and use that as a storefront, but a web address is preferable. That www.yourbook.com is part of your branding, your identity.

When you publish on Amazon, they give you a limited storefront (your landing page) and offer your book(s) globally in thirteen countries. Plus, they even convert your royalties from the different currencies into USD and deposit it into your own bank account. (not a bad deal, right?)

Yes, Amazon does take a small percentage of your royalties, but look at what they give back. You can claim a 70% or 35% royalty on e-books, your choice. Amazon does a lot of your marketing for you already. We will cover that later.

Much more of this is covered in my book: *Writing as a Retail Business*

Here is that link:

https://www.amazon.com/Writing-as-Retail-Business-Guide/dp/1530134625/

WRITING AS A
RETAIL BUSINESS
A GUIDE
S. D. ANDERSON, PhD

Writing – the WEEI method.

W – Writing to

E – Entertain

E – Educate

I – Inspire

As a Self-Publisher, it is your Duty? Moral Obligation? Whatever word you choose to use, it is that integrity that is needed to WEEI your readers – in other words – QUALITY WRITING.

You know exactly what I mean, so I won't elaborate further. When you write, place your reader in front of you, and tell him/her the story.

Glossary of Terms

Before we go any further, you need to understand the language of self-publishing.

Here is a glossary of terms that you will run into as you continue your self-publishing journey.

Glossary of terms

K.D.P. – Kindle Direct Publishing. An Amazon company for authors and publishers to publish their e-books worldwide for free, to be read electronically on Kindle, Nook, e-readers and other electronic devices. (tablets, computers, cell phones, etc.)

CREATESPACE – an Amazon company for self-publishers offering the ability to create print books, CD's, and DVD's making it easier to distribute through internet retail outlets while preserving control over your materials.

DASHBOARD - A software-based control panel for one or more applications, and for network devices. Your dashboard enables you to monitor and maintain your publications, in this instance, e-books and print books created on KDP or CreateSpace.

FORMAT - the way in which information is arranged or presented, especially in computers. A defined structure for the processing, storage or display of data. In books, the way the interior of the book is set up and presented for the reader.

TEMPLATE – a pre-set format of a document or file to be used so that the actual format does not have to be re-created each time it is to be used.

FRONT MATTER – the first section of the book in which the title, copyright, dedication, acknowledgements, preface, foreword, table of contents, and any other additional information pertinent to the book's interior is presented for the reader.

BACK MATTER- Just as front matter is what you find at the beginning of a book, back matter, simply put, is what you find at the end of a book—the sections that appear after the central story has been completed. These sections of back matter are often supplementary in nature and inform the reader about some aspect of the book, or author.

META DATA - a set of data that describes and gives information about other data. Much like an overview of the data.

COPYRIGHT - the exclusive legal right, given to an originator or an assignee to print, publish, perform, film, or record literary, artistic, or musical material, and to authorize others to do the same.

BOOK INTERIOR - The inside pages of the book where your manuscript is placed for reading. In publishing programs, there are choices as to paper color, ink color (usually black) and interior with illustrations either in color or in black and white. The most common choices are: Black ink on crème paper, black ink on white paper and color interior on white paper.

TRIM SIZE- The final size of a printed page after excess edges have been cut off is the trim size. Commercial printing companies often print several copies of one document on the same large sheet of paper.

BLEED SETTINGS - Bleed is a printing term that is used to describe a document which has images or elements that touch the edge of the page, extending beyond the trim edge and leaving no white margin. When a document has bleed, it must be printed on a larger sheet of paper and then trimmed down.

PAPERBACK - A paperback is a type of book characterized by a thick paper or paperboard cover, and often held together with glue rather than stitches or staples. In contrast, hardcover or hardback books are bound with cardboard covered with cloth.

COVER FINISH – Paperback books offer two cover finishes in this program, GLOSS and MATTE. The gloss finish is shiny and has a sleek look. The matte cover is more subdued with a non-shiny finish and a pebbly feel.

P.O.D. - Print On Demand. A book in digital format can be stored in a retrieval system and when bought, a copy is printed and sent to the customer. This pertains only to print editions, and not to e-book editions.

ROYALTIES – monies paid to the author of the sold book after printing costs and distribution costs are deducted.

DISTRIBUTION CHANNELS – are channels through which Amazon and CreateSpace distribute their inventory: Independent Book Publishing to Libraries and Booksellers, Indie Music distribution for DVDs on demand, Indie Film Distribution, and Amazon Video Direct.

A SELF-PUBLISHING SERVICE – a service to help a writer/author publish his or her manuscript on Amazon or several other sites giving the writer total control over their work. They can follow their book's progress from start, preview, proof, and final print, and then follow the book sales reports on their personal book shelf.

Programs for Writing

Which program is the best one for writing?

I usually recommend <u>Microsoft Word</u>. There are tons of writing programs, but the one most easily recognized, and easier to work with is <u>Word</u>. If you are working with another program, then I suggest that you switch your files over to this one for it will give you fewer headaches in the future if you are serious about continuing to self-publish.

I also have <u>Scrivener</u> on my computer, an excellent program to write in, but not easy to format. In fact, to format into book size, you really need the <u>Word</u> version.

<u>Word</u> is very powerful and will give you many options, especially if you intend to include small illustrations at the beginning of your chapters.

I have worked with several writers who were using other programs and formatting it into book size and dressing it up was a challenge.

MAC vs. PC

Depending what device you have, either a Mac or a PC, lap top or desk top, the writing should be done on the same program as recommended above: Microsoft Word.

I have always worked on a P.C. until I started training other writers in publishing when I discovered the difference. So, to MAC users, use whatever writing program you have and leave the formatting to Amazon for e-books. As for print books, to establish your size for your book, you may want to consider the default paperback size as a 6 x 9 and use your A5 paper size. Because, for a print book, you send it to publish in a PDF format, the formatting stays static or the same as you intended.

On your e-book, I recommend using KDP's Kindle Create program, a free download, that will help you with the set-up.

Self-Editing and Professional Editing

Editing is mandatory for both your e-book and/or your print book.

I cannot stress how very important editing is if you want to produce a quality book. The rule is you edit until you cannot stand to look at the manuscript any more. Then you have it edited by someone else.

This can be a fellow writer, or a professional editor. Family members, unless highly qualified, should not be considered. By that, I mean a family member who is skilled in grammar, punctuation, etc. My sister, who worked for the Pentagon before she retired, tears my work apart, sometimes most embarrassingly, but she is excellent, and I do ask her to edit something for me occasionally. I love her dearly, so I don't impose on her too often.

There are two types of editing:

<u>Line editing</u>, where your work is read line by line correcting punctuation, grammar, and sentence structure.

<u>Content editing</u> is a little more complicated. Your work is read, line by line, chapter by chapter to look for plot holes, character continuity, correct grammar, writing style, etc.

Using an on-line spell checker is not recommended as the go-to editor.

I CALL THEM HOOKS

What is A HOOK?

The HOOK is what you use to HOOK your readers, to HOOK their attention, to hopefully get them interested enough to buy your book. It is your one and only chance to "Make the Sale or Get the Job." If that sounds unusual, it isn't really, it's salesmanship.

You do have several chances to make that first impression, not unlike meeting someone for the first time. It's like a job interview, and in a way, that is exactly what is happening. Someone is interviewing you, (a potential reader), and you hope they will buy your book. (You will get the job)

The first thing they see is your TITLE.

HOOK #1 – TITLE

On Amazon or any book site, the TITLE is your first HOOK. If the Title holds no appeal to the reader, he/she will slide right by yours until he/she finds one that will catch their interest. (These are all Marketing Strategies, by the way.)

The MODERN READER or TODAYS READER is usually on their mobile device, computer, iPhone, and surfing to find something of interest. Unless they specifically know what they are looking for, they are surfing. They are already in their chosen category (Fiction, Non-fiction, Romance. Action/Adventure, etc.) That part is already accomplished.

What does your title say about your book? Does it reflect some sense of the book? Are you completely satisfied with this title? One of the benefits of Self-Publishing, especially on Amazon and KDP (Kindle Direct Publishing), is, you do have the option to make changes. Choose your title carefully so that it reflects what your book is about. If there is something about the title you aren't comfortable with, then work on making it better. Remember, this is what will attract your reader.

HOOK #2 COVER

Your potential reader likes your title, it's interesting and is a possibility. The next thing your reader looks at is your COVER. Covers that are very busy and have lots of action, illustrations, and printing, do have merits, remember, the reader is going to be looking at a THUMBNAIL, a postage stamp size of your cover, so plan accordingly. <u>Sometimes less is better</u>. The key ingredients here are; <u>book title, sub-title (if one) and Author's name</u>. These are what MUST show in the thumbnail of your cover.

There are numerous possibilities for you to consider for your cover. KDP and CreateSpace do offer Cover Creator, a program, with which you can DIY a decent cover. I have used both programs and had good results. You can also employ the services of a graphic artist who will create the whole thing for you, also which I have done for some of my books. Todd Engel has designed many of my covers. Here is his information at

You will see one of my book covers right in the middle of his banner-display. (Angels in Action)

A web-based program (free) for graphic design is Canva.com.

Here is their link:https://www.canva.com This program is free to use, and they do offer royalty free graphics. You can also purchase graphics for a very nominal fee.

HOOK # 3 YOUR BLURB.

Your BLURB is your introduction or the short paragraph that you will use for the back of your book cover or the paragraph that you will use to best describe what your book is about when you enter this information into the KDP program. This information will be what the public will read when they look at your landing page (the basic page on Amazon that has your cover thumbnail, price, and other pertinent information). KDP has already set up this page for you, free, and this is where your potential reader will be automatically forwarded to when they click on the thumbnail of your cover.

This HOOK #3, Your Blurb, should answer these questions:

WHO

WHAT

WHERE

WHEN

WHY

HOW

The blurb will be like a news story on the front page of a newspaper. It should answer those questions, in fact, that is where those W's came from (journalism).

To break that list down, let's do this:

1. WHO – the who is your main character- who are you writing this book about?
2. WHAT – is happening to this character that the reader should, or might want to identify with, to know more about (the plot)
3. WHERE – where is this taking place? in Chicago, Illinois, along the Amazon River, the Angelic Kingdom? The reader should have some point of reference.
4. WHEN – when is this happening? Years ago, right now, in the future?

5. WHY – what cataclysmic event has happened to the protagonist (hero/heroine) that you have written a story about? Why should the reader read on?

6. HOW - will it be resolved? How will this story end? Make this point like a cliff hanger to make the reader WANT to buy the book. (The Sale, or The Job.)

HOOK #4 FIRST CHAPTER

Amazon KDP offers potential readers a peek (look inside) at the first few chapters of your book, right on your landing page, which gives the reader a better idea of what your book is all about. This is a clever bit of marketing that KDP has already done for you. Your first chapter should also answer those five 'W' questions. Here is where you set up your story (plot) and characters. If they get this far, they are interested, and will probably purchase the book, if not now, then soon. KDP also offers the following, (built right into your landing page)

Read for free – Kindle Unlimited – you still get royalties for this option.

Kindle Matchbook – which ties your print and e-book together.

Buy now with one click – making this easy for the reader.

Deliver to the reader's device (iPhone, tablet, etc.)

Send a free sample

Give as a gift

Add to your list (this has a pull-down screen with the following:

Kindle Wish List (private)

Shopping list

Kindle Wish List (public)

Gift Ideas List

And finally, if none of the above work, *a Create a List option*.

So, you see, Amazon has done all this marketing for you, and obviously offers all these choices so the reader does not leave your landing page empty-handed. All very clever marketing tools, which benefits both the Author and Amazon.

E-Book Formatting

E-books are set up differently from books in print. There is less front matter because the reader is on a device and wants to get to the first chapter, the beginning of the story. Our current readers are SCANNERS rather than studious scholars. They want to read a book quickly (they are most probably reading on the run.) I try to impress that thought upon the members of the writing group.

Your e-book should have the following front matter:

1. Title Page

2. Copyright Page with disclosure and ISBN Number (Optional) Most e-books do not need an ISBN number. This page could also be in the back matter.

3. Dedication page (Optional)

4. Quote if it pertains to the story otherwise "no".

Because your book is on Amazon and they offer that "Look Inside" option, so the sooner your reader gets to your first chapter, the better the chances for the sale.

5. Body of the book

6. Back Matter…

Copyright Page – if you did not place it in the front matter

Acknowledgments

Author's Bio and photo

A list of other books by the author

A thank you page for buying the book

A list of the author's contact information (web site, blog, e-mail address, Goodreads link, Facebook link, Amazon Author Page)

A free first chapter of the sequel (if any)

Print Book Formatting

Your paperback or print book should also have structure, only a lot more and set up differently. Because your first chapter should always start on the right-hand page or an odd numbered page, the pages formatting will look like this.

1. Page one - Title Page

2. Page two - Copyright Page with disclosure and ISBN Number (CreateSpace and KDP both offer free ISBN numbers. You can use theirs or purchase your own block of ISBN numbers from this site:

http://www.bowker.com/products/ISBN-US.html :.

Page three - Dedication Page

Page four - Blank

Page five - Acknowledgements page

Page six – blank

Page seven – Quote (optional)

Page eight – Blank

Page nine – Chapter One (odd page)

Body of the book

Blank page at the end of the story or the last chapter. If the chapter ends on an even number page, add another blank page so that your back matter (author's bio) shows on an odd numbered page.

<u>Back Matter</u>:

Author's Bio and photo

A list of other books by the author

A thank you page for buying the book

A list of the author's contact information (web site, blog, e-mail address, Goodreads link, Facebook link, Amazon Author Page)

A free first chapter of the sequel (if any)

You can see the difference. It is a good idea to go to your library and look at how other print books are set up, or a bookstore like Barnes & Noble in their new book section.

Book Size (Paperback book only)

Many writers with their manuscript clutched in a sweaty hand ready to run, rarely think of what size they should make their book. This is rather important, as it decides what your book will look like when finished.

The default size for CreateSpace is a 6 x 9 format. This Blueprinting is written and formatted in a 6 x 9 format, or if I remember correctly, I used the A5 page size which comes close to a 6 x 9. (This was done for you Mac users.)

It is recommended that you go to your library (public or private) and pull out books that look like the size of the book you feel comfortable with.

Bring a small tape measure with you.

Pull out the book and measure it – top to bottom (height) and side to side (width)

The margins on this Blueprinting are 1" top, bottom, right and left. (one-inch margins all around.)

Margins for a 6 X 9 print book are:

0.75" top

0.75" bottom

0.75" inside

0.5" outside (left margin)

0.13" gutter (the space on the inside of the page to allow for the binding of the book.)

Make certain you click on Mirror Margins so that the pages will work for both pages of your book.

Your Headers and Footers are already at 0.5 so they can stay the same.

There are other variations for this but for our purposes here, let's keep it simple.

E-books are easier.

What to Do Before You Format

In a separate file that is easily accessible for you, (probably on your desktop) place the following:

1. A perfect author's bio about 2 paragraphs long and interesting to read. If you are having difficulties writing your own information, go online and research your favorite authors, read their bios and that should give you some idea of what to say. (NO copying)

2. An up to date author's photo. Important! (The reader wants to see what you look like).

3. A list of your personal links to place in the back matter of your book. Include links to your Amazon Author's Page, Face Book page, Website, Blog, Goodread's Author's page and your e-mail address. (it is recommended that you go on the Gmail site and create a new one especially for your books.)

4. Key words and categories for your book when you upload it on both Amazon and CreateSpace.

5. The blurb for the back of your book

6. You can use this same blurb for your paragraph on your Amazon book page (describing your book).

Put all this information in that file so you have it handy. Believe me, it makes your work a lot easier.

Setting Up Your Accounts

This step is one of the more vital things to carry out before you actually publish. Each account, one on KDP, and one on CreateSpace need to be set up for several reasons.

1. This account is where you want your royalties to go, so think about how you want to do this. You will be asked to give your financial information and to fill in tax information for a 1099. Personally, I have a business account with my bank and use this one. You can also use a personal bank account or a savings account.

2. This will also create your book page on KDP, and your dashboard on CreateSpace. You need both of those so that you can upload your finished formatted manuscript. Otherwise where will that be done?

The accounts on both KDP and CreateSpace will ask you for your title, and so forth down the page until you get to uploading your file and cover. You can stop here, because you will be doing that later. The best part is, you have this part ready.

Let's Talk About Covers

This is important, because it is your second HOOK!

CreateSpace has five pages of six cover templates each, that is thirty cover choices.

KDP also has several choices, although not as many as CreateSpace.

You also have the option of downloading a completely formatted cover from an outside designer.

Once inside either of these programs, there are further choices to create the perfect cover. I suggest you play with them. The absolute beauty of both these programs, you can always change anything in your book. Unlike Traditional publishing which doesn't allow much in the way of changes.

I have not used the KDP program to Create a Paperback since I wrote my book, but I have been told that you can make changes and get proofs now. When I published my book, *Creating a Paperback in KDP, A*

DIY Guide, proofs were not available nor were author copies.

A word about Author Copies:

Author copies are a valuable piece in Self-Publishing. These are copies that you can purchase from the printer for a nominal fee.

Example:

Your book is priced at $15.95 retail.

The printing costs are $3.50 per book.

That gives you $12.45 to play with.

You can purchase 10 copies of your book from the printer for $35.00 and sell them at a book signing for the full price, $15.95. You pay the bookstore where you had the book signing either a 30/70 or a 60/40 split or whatever terms you had set. The other option? Offer your book at a discount. Whatever you decide. Fun, isn't it?

Author copies are a valuable marketing tool. Be creative and see how you can use them.

This is what is meant when you have all this control over your books.

If you were with a traditional publisher, your royalties would be much less, and you would get paid quarterly.

Back to covers!

Covers are an expression of what your book is about. It is a peek inside.

You can choose to use a personal photo for your cover but make certain it is yours and you have permissions to use it if there are friends or family portrayed. It is important that you own the rights to that picture or photo.

Another thing to consider is the photo or picture should be in JPG File Format, as that is what CreateSpace and KDP will ask for.

Note:

Any pictures and photos should always be in JPG File Format for printing. Usually digital cameras will save automatically in that format.

Publishing (finally)

You have your final manuscript ready to go? It is all edited, cleaned up, no spelling errors, etc.

Now save it as (final copy) or some such title so that you always have that final in case you need to go back and make any changes. You can delete all the rest. (they are still safe because they are in your trash) The idea is to get them off your screen or desktop, so you don't become confused.

Now, do two save as files. One for KDP as a doc file, and one save as file as a PDF for CreateSpace. Save them to your desktop so that you can find them. Keep that other file folder handy so that you have easy access to your information.

Let's do the e-book first.

Open your book page, and scan down to the 'download your file here' place. Browse to your doc file on your desktop, click on it and KDP will download it, change it into their acceptable format and let you know if it worked, usually with a 'download successful' message.

Now move on to download your cover and complete that process.

Follow the prompts until you get to the part where they ask you if you want to preview your book. Follow the prompts and preview your book.

If you need to make changes, you have the final file.

Previewing

Once you have downloaded both your interior and your cover file and the program does it's hurly-gurly processing, you will receive a message asking you if you want to preview your book.

Of course, you do!

Even though you have edited it to almost extinction, do it because sometimes the print formatting does funny things.

Notice the side bar where CreateSpace tells you all the things that are wrong, check them out, because you want your book to be perfect, and so do they. This happens more with print books than e-books, and one of the reasons I suggested you keep the final copy.

Pricing

When you have all the kinks and glitches straightened out, you will move on to another screen where you are asked to price your book. The e-book we already suggested that it be placed between $2.99 to $4.99.

If you go too high, Amazon has a built-in indicator that will give you a price that they have found is the best one based on their past sales and what the market is paying for a book that is like yours. My suggestion is to go with what they suggest, as they have the stats to back up their suggestion.

Paperbacks are a different story. Your research should have given you an idea of where books like yours are priced. Rule of thumb: page numbers are a direct indicator.

Under 100 pages: up to $9.99

100 to 150 pages - $10.99 to $11.99

160 to 200 pages - $11.99 to $12.99

201 to 250 pages - $12.99 to $13.99

251 to 300 pages - $14.99 to $15.99

And up.

These might be a little low, so you might want to check the current market and do your own research. The idea is to sell your book, not to have it commit suicide.

Marketing

The big boo-hoo! Writers and Authors have such a challenging time with this aspect of self-publishing, (me especially) I am the classic example of "Let me write my books, do I have to market them, too?"

The answer to that is "YES"

What you are reading here is a marketing tool.

Self-publishing is a lot more than just publishing a book. I learned that early. To become successful, you must learn a new set of skills.

The Art of Selling.

Yes, you need to become a salesperson. There are thousands of ideas, methods, and techniques to show you how to do that, and many people who can show you the way. (I am not one of them.)

This is a world I will urge you to explore on your own, HOWEVER, here are some steps you can take to ensure that your book does sell.

I call it, A PLAN FOR EACH BOOK

A Plan for Each Book

As I was doing my own business plan (Angelic Communications) I wanted to take a good look at each of my books and check them out to analyze why some of them were selling and others were sitting on the screen not doing anything.

Using 3 x 5 cards again or a plain sheet, I used one card per book and did a checklist for each one. (Hint: you can also use this form directly on your computer and keep it active in a file somewhere. I recommend a file for each book.)

Also: You can put all this information and your goals up on a calendar. I have post-it notes on the wall above my work station where I can see and reference them.

Here it is:

BOOK: (You fill in the name of your book here.)

____

CHANGE THIS TITLE?

Does this book need a title change? If it is in print, you can do this by creating a second edition and going through the print process again. If you are publishing digitally, you only need to make those changes in your Microsoft Manuscript saving it as a second edition. If you publish through Amazon.com and their KDP program, you have a dashboard and can make those changes easily, BUT I would wait until I had gone through the entire checklist before dashing off to make any changes there or to any other site.

Another consideration is:

does this title reflect what your book is about?

Example:

Crystal Grids for Light Bodies. The 12 Helixes.

I thought that was a great title, but no one was interested. I had had one purchase in several months. My other Crystal Grid books were doing well. I decided to change the title and the cover making it reflect what the book was really about. I changed it to *Crystal Grids – Activating the 12 Strands of DNA*. Here are the two covers and the cover changes.

I asked Todd Engel (My cover guru) to make the changes and to simplify the cover. He is truly remarkable. I love his work

http://www.toddengelengelcreative.com .

Another consideration for the best title is to Google it to see if there are other books out there with the same title. Do the same on Amazon under both the print and the e-book section.   In another word, do your 'research' or 'homework' again.

COVER

Do you think a new cover will enhance the book? If you made a title change, then you do need a new cover. Not sure? Do some research; check out covers in the same categories and see what is selling and what would easily adapt to your book text. This is like buying and wearing a new outfit.

If you cannot afford a professional designer, you can use www.canva.com or another free or almost free program. I have used this program for several of my covers and the process is very simple. A key point to remember is - your cover is the first thing a reader sees and uses to push that buy button.

Your cover is the outfit on the dressmaker's dummy in your store window.

PRICING

Use the same considerations as above. See where the other books in your category are priced. Any shop owner knows that price comparison is a necessary decision. This also implies that you don't have to follow the pack or get into a price war. You want to give your readers honest value for honest monetary compensation.

Unless you are doing a marketing countdown or some sort of offer, personally, I don't recommend selling your book for free unless you have three or four others in a series. Then "free" is your choice. Some authors do this and again, it's their choice.

From a retail standpoint, a shop owner rarely or never offers his merchandise for free. Store owners may offer Marked Down or on Sale, but never for free.

Amazon offers a countdown marketing program for your books, which I have used with some success.

They also offer another for a free book but even that has its limitations. I offer my *Tuk-Tuk the Rabbit* for free during the Easter season, and can offer it for five days. Amazon is a retailer and very savvy in offering merchandise.

I have been with Amazon since 2010 and personally, I am pleased with the way they operate and again, personally feel that my books have done very well with them.

CATEGORIES

Have you placed your book in the right categories? Sometimes a change here is all that is needed to boost sales. Again, do your research. See what categories other books like yours are in and their ranking. Be honest, make certain you are comparing book content and not what you want yours to be. Ask yourself, is my book really like this one? Should it be in this category? Should you do more research until you are certain this is where your book belongs?

When I went back to review where I had initially placed a few of my older titles, I was appalled. What stretch of my imagination dared me to do that? Also, remember, change! Amazon is adding new categories constantly as demand requires because of their relentless research. As more readers have access to e-books, their searches, and selections change. Remember, not everyone will want to read your books, so your selections here are of the most importance. You want to make certain your books are available for your potential readers to find, consider, and purchase.

KEY WORDS

Such an important aspect of what you say about your book. Key words are important and keep your book up front for the search engines. Yes, we still use those. You can use phrases, and again do your research. Amazon gives you so many choices. Make certain you are in the Kindle e-book section of Amazon if that is where your book is to be presented.

http://keywordtool.io/ is a free online tool that you can use to determine where your book should be and the keywords that are in searches. Your title and your book blurb should have all the keywords you really need and should be the ones prominent in a keyword search.

CONTENT

Does the story or the content need to be re-edited? Many times, after a book is published, the author thinks of changes … we all do it! I have re-published the thinking or thought book four times, each with a different title and upgrading the content.

1. The 7 Second Thought
2. Changing your life with the 7 second thought
3. Thinking Your Life – The 7 second thought
4. What Are You Thinking? Your Thoughts Create Your Life.

Currently, I am considering another edition for this book being more specific. The possibilities are endless. I do hope you can see that. How about the content of your book? The more we write, the better our skills become. Books that you wrote several years ago are probably not the same caliber of writing as your books are now. Check them out to see if I am right!

AUDIO BOOK

Is this another format you might want to consider? I love audio books and have a very selective library of books from Audible.com on my Smartphone. Audible.com is another Amazon company. Listen to a few or try their introductory free offer and see if you like them. From the first few minutes, I was hooked and could visualize most of my books in audio form. What fun. I have made several attempts at creating one myself and that was even more fun.

TRANSLATION

Can you see this book published in another language?

PUBLISHING E-BOOKS

Here is where you decide if you want to use a service for publishing your books or do it yourself. There are two services that I know of, probably more: Smash Words and Draft2Digital (D2D). As more self-publishers come into this Indie arena, these services will become extremely popular. I am currently using D2D and find them tremendously helpful and user friendly. I picture this service much like my personal agent. I give them the book and they send it out to the different sites: Amazon KDP, Kobo, iBook, Nook, Scribed, Inktera, and Tolino. Yes, they do take a small percentage, but you must make that decision, and that is only when the book sells.

I don't want to think of the time it would take me to do all of this individually. Also, just to keep track of this is a nightmare. When would I write?

PRINTED EDITION

This is your decision. If you have a book in your inventory and want to create a print edition, that is up to you. I would recommend BookLocker for their Print on Demand books (which I have used) or CreateSpace (which I have also used).

SERIES

If you have written several books in a series, then you might want to consider publishing them as a 'bundle' or offer the first one in the series free so that the rest will automatically be purchased by the reader. This will be covered under Marketing Strategies.

FREE SITES

I will list a few sites you can tap into to offer your book for free:

Freebooksy.com

BookGorilla.com,

Booksends.com

There are hundreds more, I am certain, all that is needed is to Google them... I have used Amazon's KDP promotional offers and had a lot of my books downloaded globally. That was fun to watch...

More Marketing Strategies

This area is very important. Writing and Publishing are only half of the story. Here are some of the key ingredients you really should have.

1. **Website** – this is your store front. Amazon does a nice store front on your Author Page

2. **Blog** – This is your branding – who you are and what you offer

3. **Podcasts** – More branding, only a little more personal (your voice)

4. **Social Media** - Your audience, and your readers.

5. **Facebook** – Author's page Another store front in another location.

6. **Twitter** – More audience, only a faster pace and condensed version.

7. **Google+** - More audience for branding.

8. **Good Reads** – Another place for branding, except they are already avid readers.

A Business Plan for your Books

(Excerpt from the book)

WRITING AS A RETAIL BUSINESS

A Business Plan Guide

Business Plan for:

____

Year: ___________________________

.

Note: You can begin at any month if you have just made the decision and want to get started. Most business start their year, fiscal or otherwise, in either January or June. At this point, you should have a name for your business and would insert it here and the year

Yearly Plan Overview:

____

Your yearly plan can be as detailed or as loose as you want. I prefer to do a yearly overview and then plan month by month. You can list your monthly plans (loosely) here. Again, I use 3 x 5 cards for each month, usually setting the details for each month detailed book by book.

Here is where you can get into particulars. I prefer to write the cards usually at the beginning of the month, to include what I didn't finish last month and bring that forward. The cards stay right on my computer desk where I can see them daily as a reminder. It is also a promising idea to list your goals for each month on this sheet as you will probably file it away somewhere to be viewed again at the end of the year.

Make sure each card and each monthly plan begins with

MY INTENT IS TO ACCOMPLISH THE FOLLOWING THIS MONTH:

or however you wish to word it.

Yearly Plan by the month:

January:

____

February:

____

March:

____

____

____

____

April:

____

____

____

____

May:

____

____

____

____

June:

____

____

July:

August:

September:

October:

November:

____

____

____

____

December:

____

____

____

____

Now that you have LOOSLY written those goals, you can move on to the next step:

FINANCIAL

Financial goals can be anything. Let your imagination soar or be realistic, but never limiting yourself!

Remember, you are responsible for your success! Again, those $$$ goals can be listed on the back of your 3 x 5 cards for each month. That way, you can track your progress. . . . No room here to list this unless you prefer to do that. Use the monthly goals above to pencil those in.

Next step:

PRODUCTION

Production goals can be anything from one manuscript to 12. That is your choice. If you are self-publishing digitally, then one book a year is not uncommon. To write, draft, edit, re-write, re-write again, process through your beta readers, final edit, then a year is not unusual. If you plan to create audio books from the manuscript, that may take 3 to 6 months. Having them translated into another language is also realistically within that 6 months to a year framework. Finishing a book-in-progress can be listed here. Again, these can be listed on your month-by-month cards. I am currently using a calendar for this, as I can see the overall picture better.

INVENTORY

This is the perfect time to take a good long look at your current inventory to determine what is selling, what isn't, and what should be done about it. Digitally, just to change categories may work better. Offering it free for 2 or 3 days is another option. A new updated cover or a name change is another option. I have done both and found this to be effective.

PRICING STRATEGIES

Many times, just changing the prices on a book helps boost sales. If a digital book isn't selling at $4.99, do some marketing research to check where your pricing is off and make the changes accordingly. Example: your book, The Haunted House is priced at $4.99 and other books in this category (mystery, suspense,) are prices free or $2.99. What would you do? Unless you have a series of books, I feel that it is not a good strategy to offer your books for free. You are running a business. Readers will download free books because they feel they are getting a bargain. Stores rarely offer merchandise for free unless they have a specific strategy planned; which brings us to the next segment.

MARKETING STRATEGIES

These are not the same as pricing strategies. Marketing strategies are the how-to you will use to present your books (inventory) in your store front.

Store Front is your personal or business website – your blog or your podcast. If you do not have any of these, then you might want to add one or all of them to your business plan over the next year.

1. Website – This is a priority. It is your store front.

2. Blog – This is also a priority for your store front. Consider it one of your advertising mediums.

3. Podcasts – Another advertising medium.

4. Facebook – Social media is a great way to put yourself out there. You can do your own personal face book authors page.

5. Twitter – Another social media.

6. Google + - Social media. I have a page but have not explored the full potential here.

PROMOTIONAL PLANS

These are the plans that you will use to promote your individual book. These plans can be any time length from 2 day free campaign to a 6 month strategy plan.

Again, I use 3 x 5 cards for this and write it on my wall calendar. Personally, one book at a time works better unless you have a series, then you can work your strategies and promotions from them.

I have a book that is currently in print. It is sitting dead in the water. This book sits with my publisher and is not moving. I am writing the sequel and will release that one probably in June (mid-cycle). Before I do that I will drop the book from my publisher and bring it over into my store front to begin the pre-publication campaign for the sequel.

TARGET AUDIENCE

Has your target audience changed? Are there new ones where you feel your book may do better, reach more customers? Final question: do you know who your target audience is? These are your readers. Readers today are very eclectic and will read from a wide variety of genres; whatever suits their fancy at the present time. Are your books in the correct genre? Here is another way to analyze where your books are selling.

CUSTOMER CONTACT

This is your e-mail list. These are the readers who like you and want to hear more from you about your books and what you are writing. This is referred to as GREAT CONTENT. If you don't stay in touch with these readers, and offer them GREAT CONTENT, then they will find another source. Here is where you offer free information and engage your e-mail customers. This list is your gold mine. Treat it accordingly. Offer GREAT CONTENT and you will have loyal readers anticipating your next offering. Remember that it must be something they can put into use for themselves or inspire them.

WRITE to EDUCATE, ENTERTAIN AND INSPIRE!

NEXT REVIEW OF THIS PLAN:

____

Benefits of Self-Publishing

When you decide to self-publish your manuscript, you have made the decision to have COMPLETE CONTROL of your work. Everything you do with that work, (now and future) is in your hands.

You decide what the book looks like, (the formatting), the cover, and all the physical properties of that work.

You can and should copyright it. (second page after the front cover) Use the copyright symbol (look under insert on your ribbon and search for the symbol ©) Easy. You can follow this up by sending your completed manuscript to the Copyright Bureau. It takes about 16 weeks to receive your confirmation back. Find all that information here:

https://www.copyright.gov/

When you self-publish, you have several options to consider.

1. You can create an e-book

2. You can create a paperback book

3. You can create an audio book

4. You can have the book translated into several languages. German, Mandarin, and Portuguese, are the prime languages now.

5. You can create it in a podcast by chapter

6. You can offer it to magazines as a series

7. You can create a sequel or series of the book.

I think that gives you an idea of the possibilities one book has.

More Benefits of Self-Publishing

Quote from Wikipedia

*"**Speed.** An author finds out right away whether a book is a hit with readers; there is not a six-month or longer delay typical with an established publisher since the usual back-and-forth steps with a publisher are bypassed. It is possible to release a book within a few weeks after it's finished.[41] Further, it is possible to avoid the lengthy process of trying to find a literary agent to secure a publishing contract.[71]*

***No start-up costs**. Manuscripts uploaded to KDP or Smashwords typically do not incur any fees.*

***Freedom to begin the next book**. An author can self-publish and then begin work on the next project, potentially being more prolific, although this presumes that the first book won't need any marketing effort.*

***A greater share of royalties**. Self-published authors earn four to five times more per unit than if an author* *works with a traditional publisher,[5] sometimes 70% of the sale price.*

Pitch books straight to the readers*. There is no intermediary censoring what might be shown to the public. The route to readers is more direct."*

Another quote from a famous author.

"With self-publishing you don't waste your time trying to get published, which can take years of query letters and agenting, and all this stuff. You go straight to the real gatekeepers, which are the readers. If they respond favorably and you have sales, you can leverage that into a writing career. If they don't, you write the next thing. Either way you're not spending your time trying to get published, you're spending your time writing the next work.

— *Hugh Howey, author of Wool*[46]

The Good, The Bad and The Ugly

<u>The disadvantages of self-publishing</u>

You might as well have the whole story. (sigh)!!!

Another quote from Wikipedia

"There are significant challenges to self-publishing as well.

Most self-published books sell few copies. *Some estimates are that they sell fewer than 100 to 150 copies;[7] another estimate is that most sell fewer than 250 copies.[22] However, it should be noted that the vast majority of books promoted by traditional publishers fail as well.[50] Still, the overwhelming odds are that any self-published book will be ignored and end up in the "digital slush pile."[16]*

Authors must spend much time marketing their books. *Authors must work hard to market their books, which is a task that many authors are not skilled at or willing to do.[20]*

Crowded landscape. There is much competition and it is difficult to get one's book to be noticed in a glutted market.[23] Big publishers have much better prospects for getting attention for a book.[35]

Lack of prestige. A book from a traditional publisher still has a lot of cachet in that it has been vetted by editors, which gives it a "stamp of approval."[71][2]

Hard to get into bookstores. Big bookstores rarely take self-published books, and if they do, they want 50% of the sales price.[2] Publishers have established distribution channels to make this easy.

Difficulty getting reviews in the mainstream press. It is difficult for self-published books to be reviewed in newspapers and magazines. The media favors books from traditional publishers before giving reviews.[2][98]

Having to spend time marketing the book. One self-published author in Britain was working "14 hour days", spending months promoting her book Only the Innocent; while she eventually made it to the UK

Kindle bestseller chart, Rachel Abbott still has difficulty getting the publishing world to take her book seriously.[99] Another writer, Ros Barber, thinks self-publishing is a "terrible idea for serious novelists" since the requirements of marketing and promoting a book will prevent one from writing, and he continues to recommend the traditional approach.[98]

Self-published books usually ineligible for prizes. *Books are not eligible for major prizes such as the Hay festival, the Booker, the Baileys, the Costa and the Man Booker, and literary novels need these prizes to become a bestseller.[98] However, there are signs that this is changing as more books become self-published."*

Now that I have given you the dark side of self-publishing, here are some statistics that you may want to look at before you make the final decision to self-publish or not.

The Author Earnings Report. This report is published every two years. We shall see an up-to-date one soon.

http://authorearnings.com/report/february-2016-author-earnings-report/

http://authorearnings.com/report/february-2017/

Congratulations! I wish you well and happy self-publishing!

Before We Say Adieu…

I would love to help you get that first book formatted and published. Once you learn how to do it, the second and successive books are easier.

I am creating several detailed step-by-step courses to help writers who are serious about starting this new career.

If you feel that this would be of interest, please sign up on my website to become a charter member of the Audacious Academy. A charter member gets the exclusive info first. It isn't accessible to anyone else.

Here is my contact information if you need to speak with me directly:

audacious-publisher@gmail.com

My website:

www.audacious-publisher.com

My blog: (you can also access this through my web site)

There, I've said it all!

I hope to see your e-mail address on the Audacious Academy list as a charter member.

Happy writing and publishing!

Sharon D. Anderson

Cape Cod, Massachusetts

April 2018

Thank you

for buying my book. I appreciate your consideration and hope that it has been helpful to you on your self-publishing career.

Could you please leave a brief review on the site where you bought this book? Reviews help other writers decide if the information is helpful.

 Huge Hugs

Sharon

AVAILABLE IN PRINT ** starred title

Visionary Fiction

Atlantis – The Final Days**

Angels in Action

What Should You Do with Your Life?

Stones and Bones**

Something Sinister**

Visionary Non-Fiction

Creating Crystal Grids**

Sacred Grids**

Crystal Grids for Light Bodies

What Are You Thinking? **

Cosmic Blueprinting**

Raising Your Energy**

Body Blogs for Health**

<u>Children's Book</u>

Tuk-Tuk the Rabbit

<u>Spiritual Guidelines Series</u>

Prosperity Workbook

Remarkable Relationships

To Your Health**

Everyone is Evolving

<u>ON WRITING</u>

Writing as a Retail Business**

Creating a Paperback in KDP**

E-Book to Paperback CreateSpace Edition**

Blueprinting for Successful Self-Publishing**

Sharon D. Anderson, PhD, RMT

Sharon is an Author/Publisher, dedicated to her craft for more than 30 years. Writing in her genre, Visionary Fiction and Non-Fiction, all her books, websites and blogs merge a far-seeing perspective of New Age and Ancient Wisdom from Eastern and Western Philosophies.

She is a member of both the Cape Cod Writer's Center, the Alliance of Independent Authors, and Visionary Fiction Alliance. She recently founded the Cape Cod Writer's Studio which meets weekly in Dennisport, where she teaches members how to self-publish their work, supporting them on their paths to publication in the digital world.

Here is the link to her Amazon Authors Page:

https://www.amazon.com/author/andersonsharon

Her Good Reads Author Page:

https://www.goodreads.com/angelicomm

E-mail: sdanderson.books@gmail.com

Her Blog/website: https://www.audacious-author.com

NOTES

NOTES:

9 781717 233981